D1568390

The Library of Higher Order Thinking Skills™

Strategies for Analysis

Analyzing Information for Classroom, Homework, and Test Success

Katherine White

rosen central™

The Rosen Publishing Group, Inc.,
New York

Published in 2006 by The Rosen Publishing Group, Inc.
29 East 21st Street, New York, NY 10010

First Edition

Library of Congress Cataloging-in-Publication Data

White, Katherine, 1979–
Strategies for analysis : analyzing information for classroom, home-work, and test success / Katherine White.— 1st ed.
    p. cm. — (The library of higher order thinking skills)
Includes bibliographical references and index.
ISBN 1-4042-0470-9 (lib. bdg.)
ISBN 1-4042-0653-1 (pbk. bdg.)
1. Critical thinking—Handbooks, manuals, etc. 2. Test-taking skills—Handbooks, manuals, etc.
I. Title. II. Series.
LB1590.3.W53 2006
370.15'2—dc22

                                                                    2004030031

Manufactured in the United States of America

On the cover: Portion of *The Thinker* by Auguste Rodin.

Contents

INTRODUCTION

Y ou may not be aware of it, but you probably already know something about the strategy of analysis. Perhaps your teacher has asked you to clip an article from a newspaper and then write a short essay analyzing what the article says. Or perhaps you've been asked to choose a book and then write a report on what the book is about. Maybe your teacher also asked that when you write the book report, you cite outside sources to support your opinions. These are all examples of analysis. Your teacher gives you these assignments so you can learn how to analyze.

Analysis means to break down information into its parts and to see how those parts work together. This can range from looking at a math problem and figuring out how to solve it to figuring out what a vocabulary word means. As you will see throughout this book, analysis is a step-by-step process. Once you learn the process, you can analyze information on any subject.

In many ways, analysis is like detective work. While a detective analyzes clues to solve a crime, a student analyzes small pieces of information in order to understand and master the subject he or she is studying. At times, analysis can be challenging. You may find that there is too much or too little information or that you don't have the right kind of information to do a thorough analysis. This book focuses on the fundamentals of analysis so you will know how to deal with these challenges. Then you'll be better able to move forward and complete your homework or to get a great grade on a test.

Overall, your ability to analyze information is a key part of becoming a better thinker, a more successful student, and a more informed person who is capable of making smart choices both in and out of the classroom. Right now, you may worry that analysis sounds too hard. But remember, the key to analysis is to simplify information—to break down information into smaller, more manageable parts—so you can better understand the big picture. That's exactly what we'll do in this book.

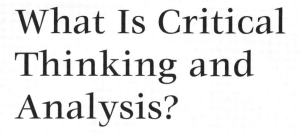

What Is Critical Thinking and Analysis?

Imagine you are working on a homework assignment and you suddenly feel stressed. Let's say your homework is to answer fifteen math problems that are similar to the ones your teacher demonstrated in class. At the time, you took notes and thought you understood, but now you cannot get through the first problem much less do all fifteen. You feel overwhelmed. You ask yourself, how do I begin this assignment?

Hopefully, after a few minutes you:

1. Go back and study your notes.

2. Read the chapter of your math book that explains similar problems.

3. Compare and contrast the different problems in the book and your notes to the math problems given to you for homework.

If you take those first three steps, you will most likely work through your first homework problem, then the second, until you finish the entire assignment. On top of just completing your homework, you also did some excellent critical thinking.

Critical Thinking

Critical thinking is the ability to understand and think through problems and challenges. Critical thinking skills allow you to use critical thinking successfully and quickly in any situation, whether you are doing your homework or taking a test. There are many types of critical thinking skills, but the six most basic skills are recalling

Did You Know? In many ways, the origin of critical thinking goes back nearly 2,500 years ago to a great thinker and philosopher named Socrates (470–399 BC). Socrates believed that a person needed to be able to think rationally and understand information. His search for critical reasoning inspired him to devote his life to teaching and writing about the subject. Luckily, a lot of research has been done in the past 2,500 years, so you can find answers about critical thinking more easily than Socrates did.

knowledge, comprehension, application, analysis, synthesis, and evaluation. These skills are also known as higher order thinking skills.

Introduction to Analysis

From the title of this book, you know we are going to focus on analysis. As you see from the previous list, analysis is just one part of critical thinking. However, analysis is one of the most important skills you can have both in and out of the classroom. Interestingly, you are already analyzing information all the time. You analyze when you are choosing which outfit to wear to school in the morning. You analyze when you are playing any kind of sport and when you are reading. You are even analyzing when you are talking about music. Think about it: you tell a close friend that you like a particular song, and when he asks why, you recite a few lyrics and then explain what you think they mean. That's analysis.

There is a difference, however, between analyzing which outfit to wear and analyzing two chapters of your history book and then writing a short summary of what you think life would be like in the Middle Ages. The difference is pretty clear, right? When choosing an outfit, you're analyzing simpler information than when you're doing your history homework. When you're writing an essay, your mind has to work harder to choose and explain the right answer.

Did You Know?

Every job requires some knowledge of analysis. Here are just a few examples:

- Tax accountants **analyze** their clients' financial information in order to determine how much tax they owe.

- Auto mechanics **analyze** the parts and systems of a car in order to determine why the car is not working properly.

- Doctors **analyze** their patients' symptoms in order to treat diseases.

- Civil engineers **analyze** traffic patterns in order to determine where it is necessary to build new roads.

Breaking Down Information

Analysis means the breaking down of information into its parts to see how those parts work together. Sometimes you analyze things without even knowing it. For example, when you read the previous sentence, your mind took in each word. Then you strung together the meaning of each word so you could understand the entire sentence.

At other times, analysis takes a little bit more work. Let's say you did not understand the previous sentence. Then you would go back and reread it. Next, you would look at each word and define it. As you defined each word, you would understand the meaning of the sentence a little bit more, until you finally understood the whole thing. That's exactly what analysis is—breaking down information into smaller parts so you can understand the whole.

Asking Effective Questions

Analysis often begins with asking effective questions. In general, you should always start questions with who, what, where, why, when, or how. Questions that begin with these words require an answer that is more complex than just yes or no and can help you draw connections between ideas. In contrast, stay away from yes or no questions because you will most likely hit a dead end once you answer yes or no.

A good way to check if you're asking an effective question is to ask yourself:

1. Does my question make the information more meaningful?

2. Does my question make the information easier to understand?

3. Does my question increase the number of meaningful connections?

For example, imagine that you are analyzing an episode of your favorite TV show. A question you might ask would be: why did the main character choose to lie to his best friend? This question meets all the requirements of an effective question. It makes the information (the episode) more meaningful and helps you better understand the character. The question also helps you make meaningful connections to other parts of the episode, such as how the character's lie affected other characters.

Analysis Is Practiced Everywhere

Analysis is performed in most areas of life, which is why there are so many different types of analysis. Businesses use profit analysis to figure out how much money they are earning on the products they sell. Scientists perform data analysis so they can analyze the observations they make during an experiment. The police force uses strategic analysis to track crime trends so they can better understand criminal activity. Analysis applies to almost every scope of life because analyzing information can only lead to a better understanding of what someone is interested in or studying. As a student, you will mainly

Answer It!

Which one of the following is not an effective question you might ask after reading about the Emancipation Proclamation?

A) Why did Abraham Lincoln issue the Emancipation Proclamation?

B) Did Abraham Lincoln issue the Emancipation Proclamation?

C) How did the Emancipation Proclamation affect slaves in the Southern states?

Hopefully, you answered B. This is not an effective question because it can be answered quickly and easily with "Yes." It doesn't make you think about the topic in a complex way.

concentrate on critical analysis. Critical analysis means you are evaluating information using analytical skills. Chapter 2 will discuss critical analysis as well as analytical skills.

Critical Analysis and Analytical Skills

CHAPTER

2

Good students are patient thinkers. They ask powerful questions and make thorough observations. One of the ways you can become a stronger student is to learn how to do critical analysis. Critical analysis develops your ability not only to understand what you learn but also to question it—to go beyond memorizing information so you can retain, grow, and apply your knowledge.

What Is Critical Analysis?

Critical analysis means you are evaluating information using analytical skills. When you are evaluating information, you are determining its meaning and importance. No matter the subject, the point of critical analysis is to achieve a deeper understanding and a fuller appreciation of whatever you are studying. For example, your teacher may have you read a short poem in class and then ask you to explain in your own words what the poem means. In your explanation, the teacher wants you to perform critical analysis because he or she wants to know two things: (1) what you believe the poem means and (2) how you came to your conclusion about what the poem means.

Introduction to Analytical Skills

Analytical skills are the various ways that you can break things down into parts and then use those parts to understand the whole thing. Throughout the school day, you are probably asked to use your analytical skills in almost every subject you are learning.

However, not every class will use the same word for analysis. In science, you may be asked to classify different animals according to whether they live on land or in the water, or whether they breathe with gills or with lungs. In history, you may be asked to outline a chapter of your history book for homework. In math, you may be asked to divide the amount of your weekly allowance by the number of days there are in a week. In each case, you are being asked to analyze information. The first step in developing your analytical skills is to recognize the words that signify critical analysis.

Words That Signify Critical Analysis

As you will see from the following list, each word suggests that you need to utilize the information you are being presented with, whether you are evaluating, organizing, or arranging information. Overall, the words in this list suggest that you need to peel back a layer of information and look at it more closely. As a result, you are analyzing information.

break down To divide into categories.

classify To arrange in classes or groups sharing similar attributes.

compare To examine the character or qualities of, especially in order to discover resemblances or differences.

connect To place or establish in a relationship.

contrast To evaluate with respect to differences.

dissect To take apart in order to understand.

divide To separate into two or more parts, areas, or groups.

examine To look at carefully; to investigate.

explain To make something understandable.

illustrate To make clear by giving an example or by serving as an example.

order To put in order or arrange.

outline A condensed version or summary of a particular subject.

prioritize To list or rate (as projects or goals) in order of importance.

Answer It!

The following items have been **classified** together because they all share a similar trait. Can you guess what these items have in common?

- Salamander
- Puma
- Comet
- Kite

The answer is that all the items listed above have a tail.

separate To make a distinction between.

specify To name or state in detail.

Prioritizing: An Analytical Skill That Stops Procrastination

Let's look at an example of how one of the words in the previous list signifies analysis. Think back to the last time you had a lot of homework. When you sat down to work on it, did you get started right away? Or did you doodle in your notebook, call a friend, check your e-mail, or surf the Internet? Procrastination usually kicks in around the time a student feels overwhelmed. Procrastination is a long word for putting off doing something that needs to be done. Next time you find yourself procrastinating, take a few minutes to prioritize what you need to get done by making a priority list.

A priority list is exactly what it sounds like: you make a list of projects or assignments in order of their priority. However, there are ways to make priority lists so you learn the information and finish your homework with the least amount of stress.

Steps for Making a Priority List

1. Deadline is the first thing to think about when making a priority list. Assignments that are due the following day should be worked on before an assignment due next week, so place assignments that are due first at the top of the list.

2. After listing each assignment according to its deadline, figure out which one is the most difficult for you. Always place the most difficult or least enjoyable task near the top of the list. For example, if you do not like math, but you love English, then you should always start with your math homework. The reason: your mind is much more energetic and focused when you begin your homework than after you've been working on it for an hour or so.

3. At this point, your priority list should have assignments in order of their deadline and difficulty.

4. The last things to prioritize are really big assignments, such as book reports. Keep in mind that a long and difficult assignment can be broken up over the course of a number of days, or even weeks, depending on how long the report is and how much you need to research. Working on a tough assignment for twenty minutes a night will feel like much less work than sitting down to do it all at once.

5. In review, a priority list would look like this:

- Outline two chapters for history (due Monday)

- Solve twenty math problems (due Tuesday)

- Summarize a newspaper article (due Tuesday)

- Read two chapters of *Treasure Island* (due Tuesday)

- Write a report on Robert Louis Stevenson, the author of *Treasure Island* (due next Monday, work on twenty minutes a night)

Overall, by making a priority list, you accomplish two things. First, you see exactly what you

Try It!
....

Imagine that it's Monday and you've just finished dinner. You have a lot of homework this week. There's a spelling quiz on Tuesday and a big math test on Wednesday. You need to read a chapter of your history textbook by Wednesday. For biology class, you have to memorize the names of all the bones in the human body by Friday. Also, a two-page essay on the cold war is due a week from today. And finally, you have fifteen math problems due tomorrow.

On a separate piece of paper, create a priority list that will help you finish your homework on time and do your best on your tests and quizzes.

need to do and you also organize all your tasks. Second, you will most likely see that what you actually have to do is less than the amount it feels like. If you are a visual thinker, check out the sidebar "Did You Know?" on the next page to learn how to web information.

Do you also see how making a priority list is analyzing information? In this case, you are analyzing the most effective way to complete your homework. As a result, you will learn more, reduce stress, and spend less time on your homework.

Did You Know?

Have you ever heard the phrase "a picture is worth a thousand words"? A **concept map** is a method of visually representing information. Overall, the purpose of concept mapping is to see an overview of a certain topic. The map contains only the key words of an idea, but it helps you break down information into a main topic and supporting ideas.

Example of a Concept Map

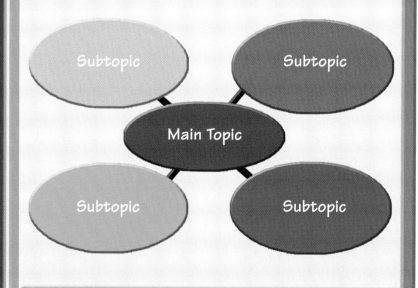

Knowing When to Use Your Analytical Skills

The "Words that Signify Critical Analysis" list on pages 15 and 16 is a great resource for knowing when to use your analytical skills, but it is not a complete list. Why not make a full list? The list would be incredibly long! As we mentioned in chapter 1, analysis is performed in so many areas of life that a full list of words could be a book in itself. The list on pages 15 and 16 contains the most common words that you will encounter in the classroom. However, as you read the rest of this book and learn more about analytical skills, you will learn to recognize words that signify analysis all on your own. Remember, words that signify analysis suggest that you need to use the information you are being presented with, whether you are evaluating, organizing, or arranging information.

3

Developing Your Analytical Skills

Analytical skills will follow you throughout the rest of your education. During middle school and high school, you will need to analyze information. If you decide to go to college or any technical school, analysis will be an important part of your learning there, too. In fact, once you finish your education and find a job, you will continue using your analytical skills because every career requires critical thinking and analysis. By learning analytical skills now, you are mastering skills that you will use throughout your life.

Now that you are familiar with critical analysis and you can recognize a variety of analytical skills, it is time to sharpen and improve these skills.

Comparing and Contrasting

Comparing and contrasting is the process of identifying how things are alike and different. Comparison refers

Did You Know?

Here are some tips on how to analyze a school text:

1. Ask yourself: what did my teacher say about this chapter or subject when it was assigned?

2. Ask yourself: what do I already know about this subject?

3. Read the title and introduction of the text.

4. Read all the headings and subheadings. If you need to, turn each heading or subheading into a question.

5. Read all the words under pictures, graphs, charts, or maps in addition to reading the main text.

6. As you read, pay close attention to all bold, italicized, and underlined words.

7. Reduce your reading speed if you do not understand some of the information, and also be sure to stop and reread any parts that are unclear.

8. Take notes on anything that is complex or hard to remember.

9. Read the summary or review if there is one, and ask yourself questions about what you learned.

to how two things are alike, and contrast refers to how they are different. There are a variety of ways in which comparing and contrasting plays out in the classroom. You can compare and contrast two movies, or you may write an essay in which you compare and contrast two events. No matter what you are comparing and contrasting, the process is always the same. First, you must gather information on two or more topics, and then you must apply what you know by analyzing how these topics are alike and different. Because there may be a large amount of information involved, this can sometimes be difficult.

Comparing and Contrasting Using Lists

One of the best ways to organize and analyze your thoughts when comparing and contrasting is to make lists. In the following sections, we will use an example of comparing and contrasting two movies about the explorer Christopher Columbus. However, you can use this method in any situation in which you are comparing and contrasting.

Step 1: Watch and Take Notes

As you watch each film, you should jot down notes about each one. Your notes should describe the main characters, the setting, and important details of the plot.

Step 2: Create Two Lists

After you watch the films, you should organize your notes by creating a list for each film. All entries in your lists should be as brief as possible. This will make it easier to compare and contrast the movies.

Step 3: Analyze the Movies

Once you create the two lists, you should compare them to see what is similar and different about the two films. This is the compare-contrast. For example, does one film show only Christopher Columbus's long journey to the new land and all the challenges he faced as the leader of the expedition? Or does one film concentrate more on how Christopher Columbus's discovery impacted the way of life for the Native Americans already living in the New World? Do both films show Christopher Columbus as a heroic explorer? Do both films show the importance of his discovery?

Step 4: Make a New List

Once you create both lists and ask yourself questions

Write It!

On a separate sheet of paper, **compare** and **contrast** yourself and your best friend. Make a list of your similarities and a list of your differences. Then, write a few short paragraphs summarizing what you found.

about the films' similarities and differences, you are ready to make a third list. This third list combines your first two lists, but it is more structured. In one column, you should list all the similarities you find between the two films. Then, in a second column, list all the differences.

Outlining: Putting the Facts in Order

An outline is a shorter, more condensed version of a particular subject. You can think of it as a road map of what you have already read or a road map of something you are going to write. An outline can help you organize your thoughts and materials, and it can also help you make connections you missed while you were reading or researching. Making an outline is also a great way to figure out what information is the most important and in contrast what information is not as essential.

Outlines are very flexible, meaning you can organize your outline depending on your needs. Are you outlining a chapter of your science book? Are you analyzing two historical events? Or are you outlining a research paper you are going to write? In any case, keep in mind that an outline should be a summary of ideas and it should always be logical. This is why there is a standard format for all outlines.

Setting Up an Outline

Setting up an outline does not have to be time-consuming, but it does have to be organized, which requires critical thinking and analytical skills. When you are making an outline, you should focus on the main ideas of the subject. Let's say you are outlining a chapter of your science book about endangered species. Below you will see a mock outline about endangered species. However, you can use this format for any subject you are outlining.

Endangered Species

I. Causes of Endangerment (main topic)

    A. Habitat destruction (subtopic)
       1. Earth has been affected by humans (details)
       2. Humans destroy forests that support animal life (details)
    B. Introduction of exotic species (subtopic)
       1. Species are introduced into new environments by humans (details)
       2. Exotic species put native species in danger by preying on them (details)
    C. Overexploitation (subtopic)
       1. Endangerment due to hunting of the species (details)
       2. Unrestricted whaling (details)

Try It!

Find an old essay, research paper, or book report. Create on **outline** that shows how you broke down the subject. Can you see any ways that you might have improved the organization of your writing? Is anything missing or out of place?

Persuasive Writing: Arguing and Supporting Your Opinion

In almost every research paper, book report, or essay you write, you will be arguing an opinion. In fact, the purpose of any analytical essay is to share your sense of what you think the text means. To express your ideas, you need to choose a point of view and write about it. Point of view, also called POV, is the position from which something is considered or evaluated. It is one of the most important parts of persuasive essay writing.

Steps to Writing a Persuasive Essay

The following steps should be used to write a persuasive essay:

1. Choose a position or POV. What problem or issue are you going to write about? A good way to

choose your position is to research the various sides of an issue then choose the POV you find most interesting.

2. Consider who will be reading your essay. Decide if you think your audience will agree, disagree, or remain neutral about the point of view. Anticipate any questions the audience may have, and make sure to address those questions in the essay.

3. Research your topic thoroughly. A persuasive essay must provide convincing evidence because you want to challenge the reader as well as help him or her understand your perspective. Many times, when you research and read up on your perspective, as well as opposing positions, you will better understand your topic and be able to better explain your opinion.

4. Organize your essay so it explains your viewpoint. Before you write, know what evidence you will include and how you are going to present it.

Analyzing an Essay

It is important to be able to write a convincing essay, and it is also important to know the right way to read other people's essays. The following step-by-step process shows you what to look for when analyzing an essay.

1. Read the essay quickly to get an idea of what it is about.

2. Next, reread the essay more slowly and carefully. Make an effort to understand the author's main point. As you are reading, look up the meaning of words that you do not recognize.

3. Once you know the main point, go back and identify the topic sentence of each important paragraph. You can often find the topic sentence by looking for the sentences near the beginning of each paragraph that state a new idea.

4. At this point, ask yourself if both sides of the topic have been presented. Has the author used evidence to back up his or her ideas?

5. Paraphrase the author's main point.

Try It!

Choose one of the longer essays in the editorial section of your Sunday newspaper. Analyze the essay by following steps 1 to 5 on this page. Pay special attention to step 4. Did the essay cover all sides of the topic? Did the essay seem to be well researched? If you answer no to either of these questions, how could the essay be improved?

The Value of Analysis

In this chapter, you learned some valuable analytical skills. Each one of these core skills will help you become a stronger student because you will be able to compare and contrast, outline, and write a persuasive essay. In the next chapter, we will focus on applying your analytical skills when taking tests.

Chapter 4

Analysis Under Pressure: Taking Tests

Almost every student, no matter what his or her age or grade, dreads taking tests. One of the main reasons students dislike test taking is the stress involved in preparing for the test as well as the stress of actually taking the test. As you have seen throughout this book, analysis plays a huge role in the classroom, and test taking is not an exception. Analysis is a large part of test taking because you must analyze each and every question on the exam. It's also a large part of preparing for the exam because you must analyze what information to review.

Preparing for the Test

Your teacher gives you tests because he or she wants to make sure you are learning the material taught in class. Therefore, studying for a test requires you to review. One of the biggest myths about studying is that the longer

Try It!

Earlier in this book, there was a list of words that signify analysis. On a separate sheet of paper, write a sample test question for the following words that signify analysis:

- compare
- contrast
- order
- break down
- explain

For example, for the word "compare," a sample test question might be:

Compare the characters Huck Finn and Tom Sawyer.

you study the better your grade will be. In truth, studying for an extremely long time actually increases test-taking stress. What really matters is the quality of your studying. To improve your test scores, review the list of Top-Notch Study Skills below:

Top-Notch Study Skills

- Ask your teacher what material will be emphasized on the test. Also find out what kind of test it will be. Is it an essay test, multiple choice, true or false, or a combination of all three?

- Study in a quiet place away from distractions. Libraries are always a good place for studying.

- Start studying days before the exam. Studying in short bursts three times during the week is much better than a long study period the night before the test.

- Always reread your class notes. Also, reread any textbook chapters that the test will cover. Review your notes periodically, then cover them up and try to summarize them in your head or out loud.

- Set a goal for yourself during each study period. Create a priority list for the topics your test will cover. (See chapter 2 for how to make a priority list.) Then, each night, cover one of the topics your test is going to be on.

- If your teacher gives you study sheets or practice exams, always be sure to complete them. These materials are great study guides.

- Go to any review sessions offered by your teacher. Ask questions about anything that is not clear to you.

Taking the Test

Once you finish studying, you should feel confident about the material. But no matter how prepared you feel before the test, you will still feel a bit of stress when it's actually time to take the test. Do not misinterpret this stress as a feeling of being unprepared, because this stress is actually a good type of stress. It helps your mind focus on the challenge of the test. Check out the Top-Notch Test-Taking Skills below to learn the best way to take a test.

Top-Notch Test-Taking Skills

- Always read the instructions carefully.

- Quickly look over the whole test before you begin to answer questions. Make sure you look at each section's point value. This helps you decide which sections you should spend the most time on. Answer the easiest questions first, then answer the questions with the highest point value.

- If you get stuck on a question, come back to it later. You might remember the answer while you're working on another question. If you aren't sure how to answer a whole question, try to answer half or part of it. Your teacher might give you partial credit.

- If you really do not know the answer on a multiple choice test and need to guess, first eliminate the answers you know are not correct, then take a guess. Sometimes, it may help to circle key words in difficult questions.

- On an essay test, take a moment to plan your writing. You can make a quick outline or sketch of what you want to say.

- Ask your teacher for clarification if you don't understand what a question is asking for.

- Leave time at the end of the test to look over your answers. Make sure you answered every question and double-check for errors.

Analyzing Test Questions

Although stress is a good thing before a test, it can also make a student feel rushed during a test. In fact, one of the most common problems for students when taking a test is that they do not carefully read the questions. This often creates problems, like misunderstanding a question, not following instructions, and even sometimes answering the wrong question.

This is why when you analyze a test question, it is important to read the question carefully. Then you should always reread the question a second time. Look for key phrases, like the words that signify analysis that you learned in chapter 2. Also, if

Did You Know?

When you figure out the meaning of a word from **context clues**, you are making a guess about what the word means:

1. If you come upon a sentence that you have trouble understanding, you should first reread the sentence and insert a different word that seems to make sense in place of the word you do not recognize.

2. Continue reading and see if the word you inserted makes sense in the rest of the sentence as well as the rest of the paragraph.

3. If the sentence does not make sense, try another word.

4. If you are still stuck, look the word up in the dictionary or ask your teacher what the word means.

you do not understand a question or a word in the sentence, you have two options. First, you can look for context clues, or you can ask your teacher to explain the question to you. There is nothing wrong with asking for him or her to rephrase the question.

Pacing Yourself During Standardized Tests

Every year, millions of American students take standardized tests. Standardized tests are a way for the local, state, and federal governments to analyze how well students are doing in schools across America. These tests are important, and many times students feel extra stress when taking them.

Taking a standardized test is not that different from taking a regular exam. The biggest difference between the two is that standardized tests are much longer than your regular exams. They also cover almost every subject you are learning. This is why one of the most important things you can do while taking standardized tests is to pace yourself. When you pace yourself, you do not think about taking the whole test all day long. Instead, you concentrate on getting through the test section by section. You can also apply all the test-taking skills you have learned throughout this chapter when taking standardized tests.

As you can see, there are many ways to decrease stress when preparing for an exam and also when you're taking one. Even though studying and taking exams is stressful, both do not necessarily have to be overwhelming experiences. Ultimately, if you use the skills described in this chapter, you will not only improve your studying and test-taking experiences, you will also improve your grade.

Wrap Up

In this book, you have learned how to analyze and use critical thinking skills. As mentioned earlier, analysis will follow you throughout the rest of your education and into the career you choose. Even though analysis in the classroom is incredibly important, it is also essential that you remember to use your analytical skills outside the classroom as well.

There are a variety of ways you can put your analytical skills to use outside the classroom. You can analyze the media, politics, your personal decisions, your favorite music, and movies. Remember, analysis is important in all areas of life. No matter the subject or situation, you can rely on analysis to help you figure out the bigger picture.

GLOSSARY

analogy An implied (unstated) relationship between two pairs of objects.

analysis The breaking down of information into its parts to see how those parts work together.

analytical skills The various ways that you can break things down into parts and then use those parts to understand the whole thing.

comprehension Grasping the meaning of something; understanding.

context What surrounds a word or passage; often it can be used to shed light on what the word or passage means.

critical analysis The evaluation of information using analytical skills.

critical thinking The ability to understand and think through problems and challenges.

critical thinking skills The skills needed to successfully use one's critical thinking.

evaluate To judge.

genre Category of artistic, musical, or literary composition characterized by a particular style, form, or content.

observation An act of recognizing and noting a fact or occurrence often involving measurement with instruments.

outline A description of a topic that highlights the most important parts.

paraphrase To rephrase another's writing in your own words.

philosopher A great thinker; someone who develops theories in a particular area of expertise.

prioritize To list or rate (as projects or goals) in order of priority.

procrastination The putting off of something that needs to be done.

retain To keep in possession or use.

signify To be a sign of.

strategy A careful plan or method.

synonym One of two or more words or expressions that have the same or nearly the same meaning.

WEB SITES

Due to the changing nature of Internet links, the Rosen Publishing Group, Inc., has developed an online list of Web sites related to the subject of this book. This site is updated regularly. Please use this link to access the list:

http://www.rosenlinks.com/lhots/stan

FOR FURTHER READING

Abbamont, Gary W., and Antoinette Brescher. *Test Smart! Ready-to-Use Test-Taking Strategies and Activities for Grades 5–12*. Nyack, NY: Center for Applied Research in Education, 1996.

Ernst, John. *Middle School Study Skills*. Westminster, CA: Teacher Created Resources, 1996.

Gilbert, Sara Dulaney. *How to Do Your Best on Tests*. New York, NY: Morrow, 1998.

James, Elizabeth, and Carol Barkin. *How to Be School Smart*. New York, NY: Lothrop, Lee, and Shepard, 1998.

Nuzum, Margaret. *Study Skills That Stick*. New York, NY: Scholastic, 2001.

Silver, Theodore. *Study Smart: Hands-on, Nuts-and-Bolts Techniques for Earning Higher Grades*. New York, NY: Villard, 1992.

BIBLIOGRAPHY

Claremont College Library. "Critically Analyzing Information." 2003. Retrieved September 22, 2004 (http://library.clc.uc.edu/ analyzinfo.html).

Cuesta College. "Academic Support Guides: Critical Thinking." 2003. Retrieved September 24, 2004 (http://academic.cuesta.edu/ acasupp/AS/400Index.htm).

Delmar College. "Persuasive Essay Writing." Retrieved September 29, 2004 (http://www.delmar.edu/engl/ wrtctr/handouts/persuasive.htm).

Eagle Hill Middle School. "Study Skills for Middle School: Reading Skills." 1998. Retrieved August 29, 2004 (http://www.fm.cnyric.org/eagle_ Hill/bowers/read.htm).

Eduscapes.com. "Critical and Creative Thinking: Bloom's Taxonomy." January 2003. Retrieved August 17, 2004 (http://eduscapes.com/tap/ topic69.htm).

Fisher, Alec. *Critical Thinking: An Introduction*. Cambridge, England: Cambridge University Press, 2001.

Human Rights Resources Center. "A Process for Analyzing Events." 2002. Retrieved August 27, 2004 (http://www.omod.no/ english/05a-documents/hrh-and-n/Part-3/ Activity_14.htm).

Lye, John. "Critical Reading: A Guide." 1996. Retrieved August 27, 2004 (http://www. brocku.ca/english/jlye/criticalreading.html).

McPherson, Fiona. The Memory Key. "Ways to Ask Better Questions." 2000. Retrieved August 28, 2004 (http://www.memory-key.com/StudySkills/asking_better_ questions.htm).

Media Literacy Clearinghouse. "Ways to Analyze." 2000. Retrieved August 27, 2004 (http:// www.med.sc.edu:1081/waystoanalyze.htm).

Middle Tennessee State University. "Survival Strategies for Taking Tests." Retrieved December 10, 2004 (www.mtsu.edu/~studskl/ teststrat.html).

Northwest Learning Grid. "Exam Techniques." 2001. Retrieved August 29, 2004 (http://www.nwlg.org/pages/resources/ knowitall/exams/examtech.htm).

Pearson Education. "Studying for Tests." 2000. Retrieved August 21, 2004 (http://www. factmonster.com/homework/studyskills4. html#tips).

Spalding, Cathy. "Top 10 Study Tips." Retrieved December 10, 2004 (http://homeworktips. about.com/cs/toppicks/tp/topstudytips.htm).

TestTakingTips.com. "Test Taking Skills, Tricks, Strategies, & Techniques." Retrieved December 10, 2004 (www.testtakingtips.com/test).

U.S. Department of Education. "Critical Analysis and Thinking Skills (CATS)." 1995. Retrieved September 21, 2004 (http://www.ed.gov/pubs/ EPTW/eptw10/eptw10f.html).

Virginia Polytechnic Institute and State University. "How to Read Essays You Must Analyze." 2002. Retrieved August 29, 2004 (http://www.ucc.vt.edu/stdysk/essays.html).

INDEX

About the Author

Katherine White is a writer and editor who has written over fifteen young adult books on topics such as education, science, and the environment. Currently, she lives in Jersey City, New Jersey.

Designer: Nelson Sá; Editor: Brian Belval